PRIDE FLAGS
LGBTQ COLORS

DECORATIVE CRAFT PAPER

8 x 8 | 12 SHEETS 6 DESIGNS

CUT LUV
PAPERS

REMOVE WITH SCISSORS

AF261309

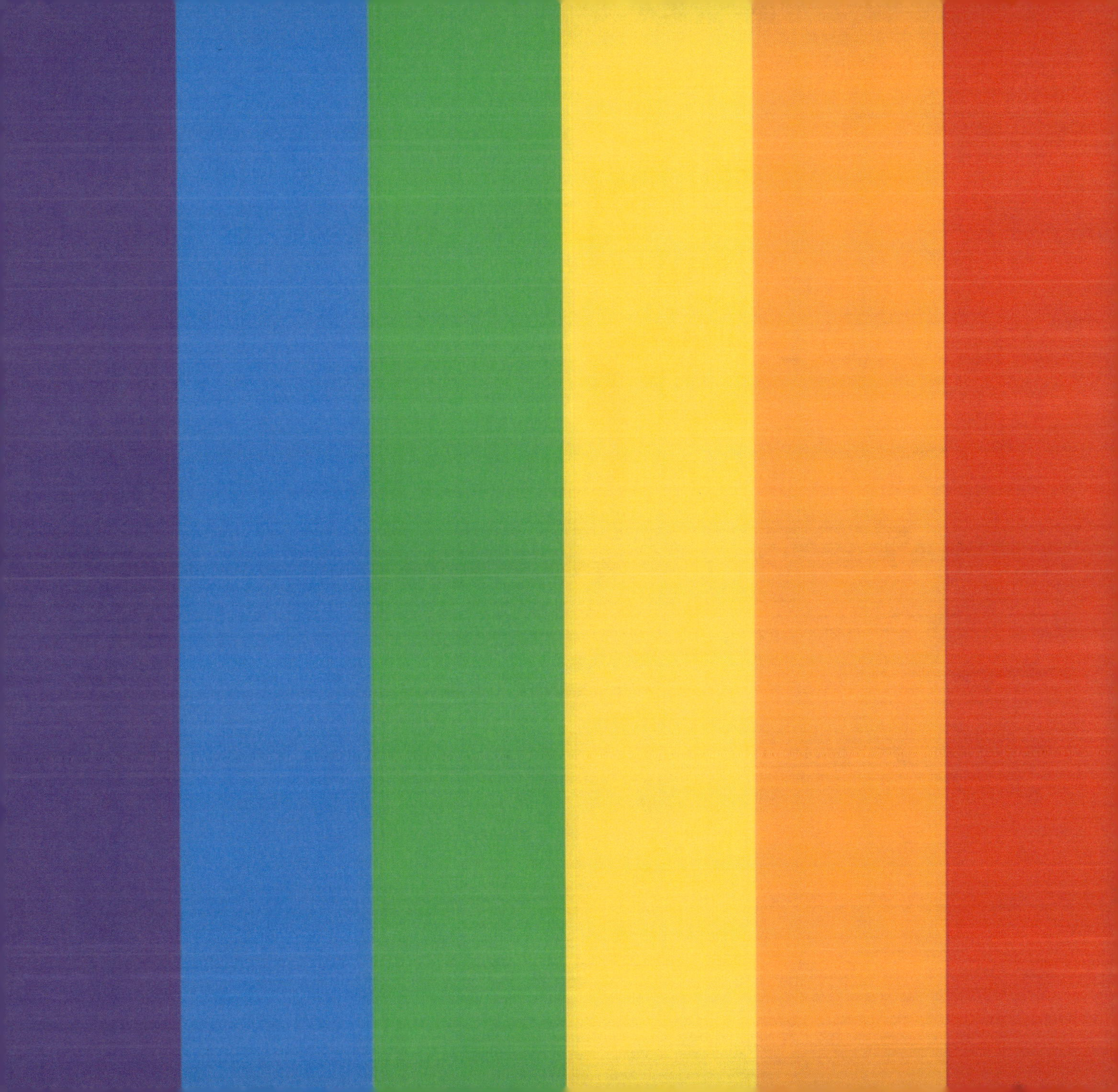

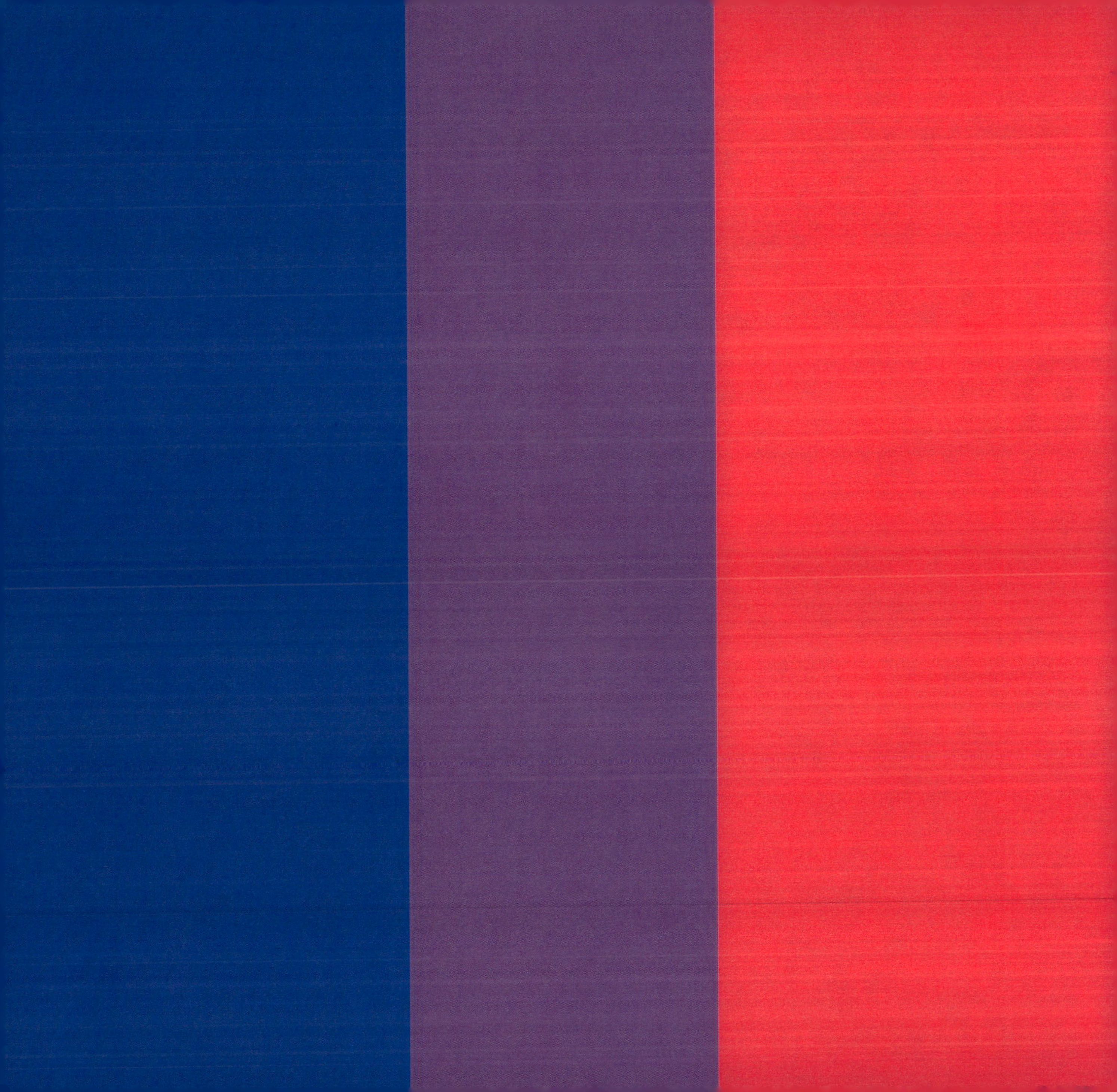

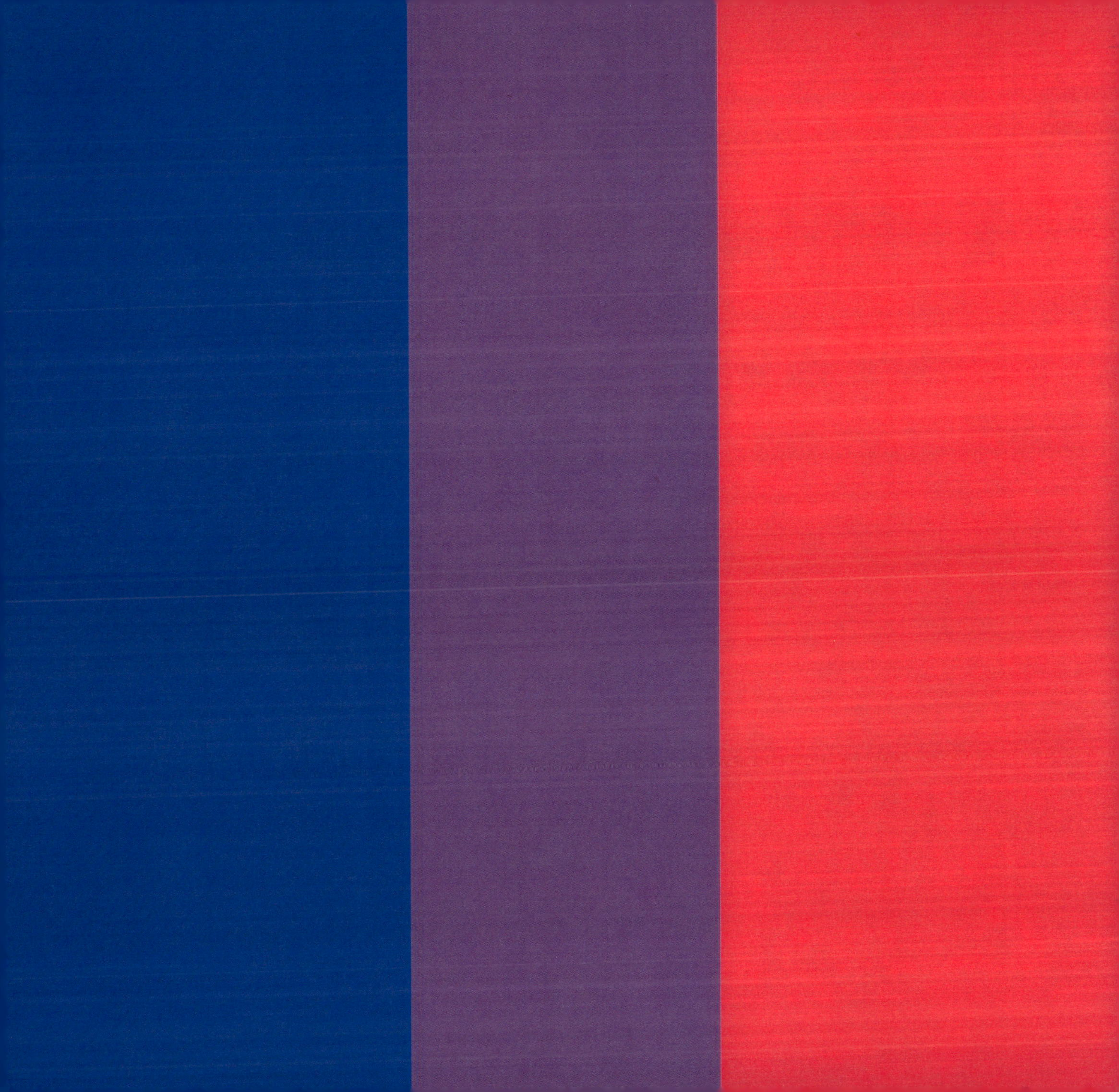

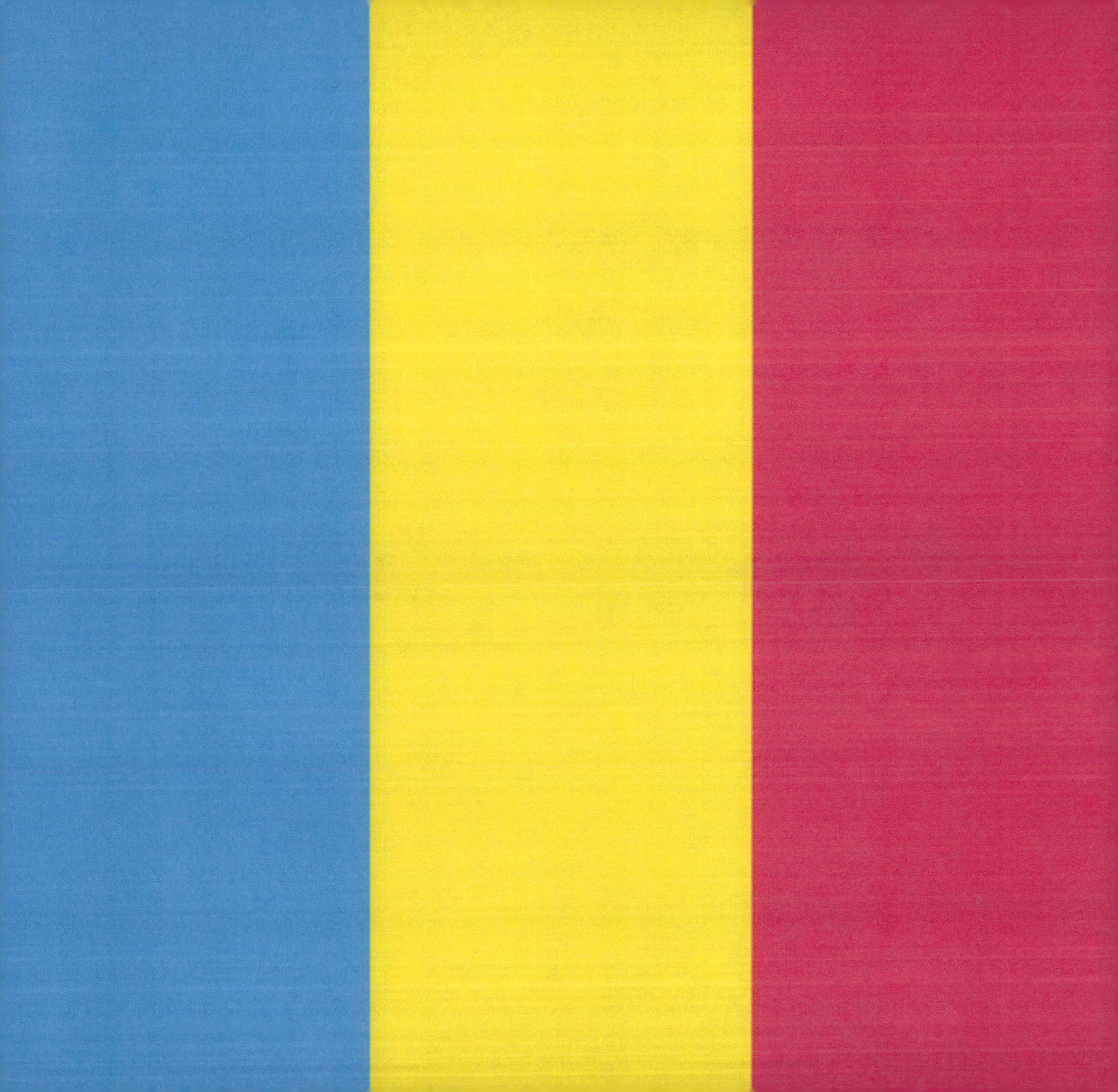

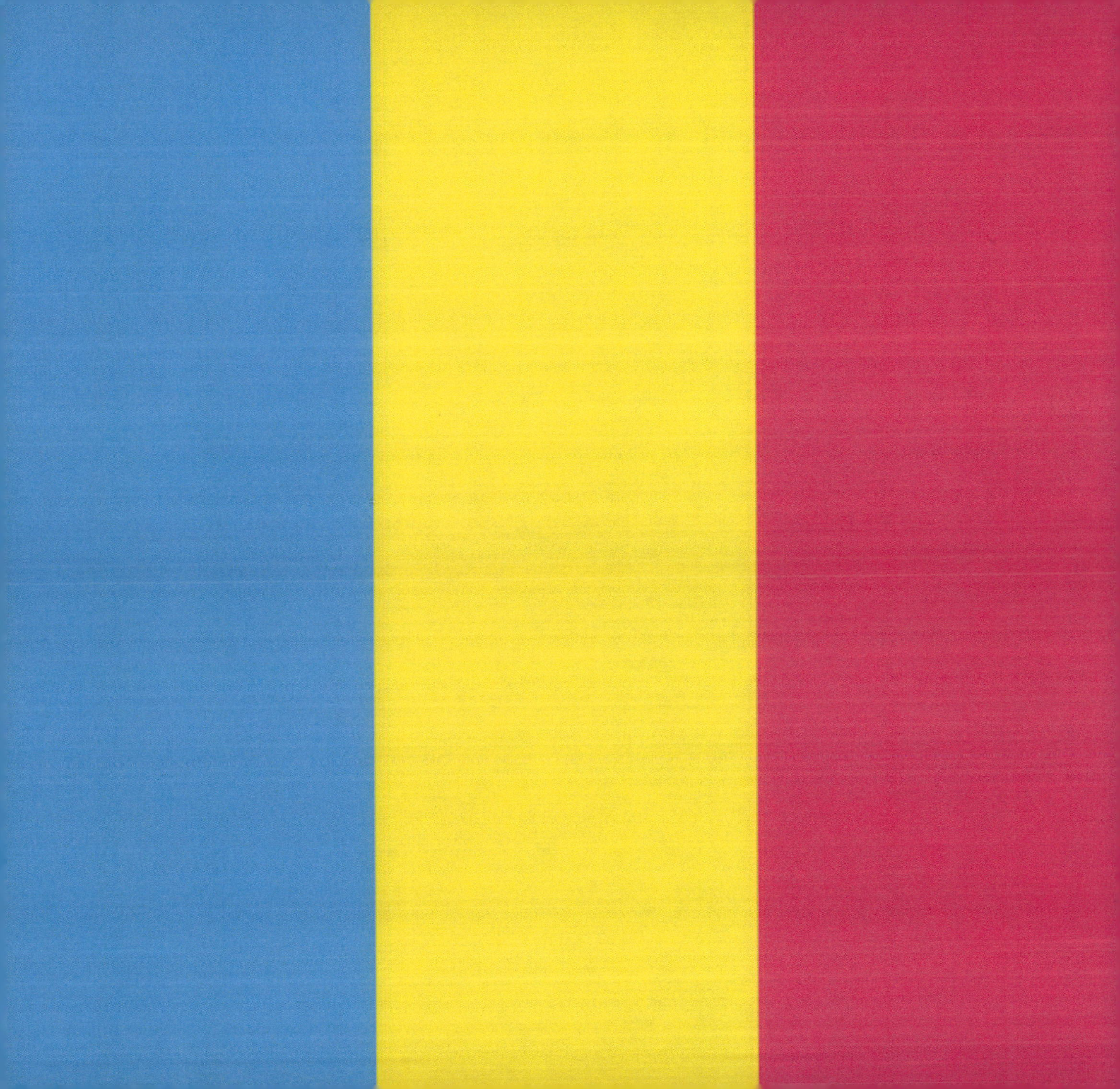

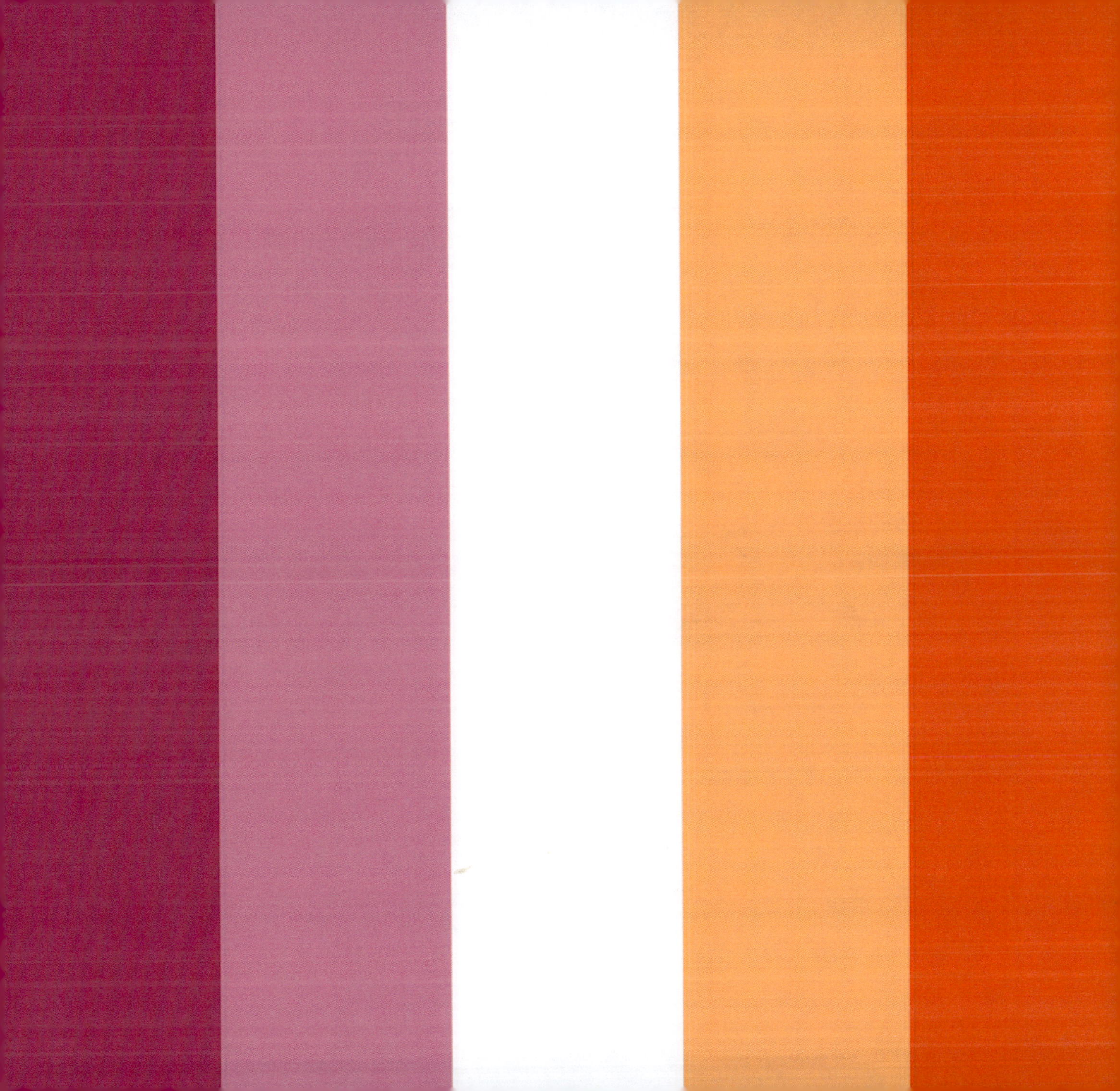

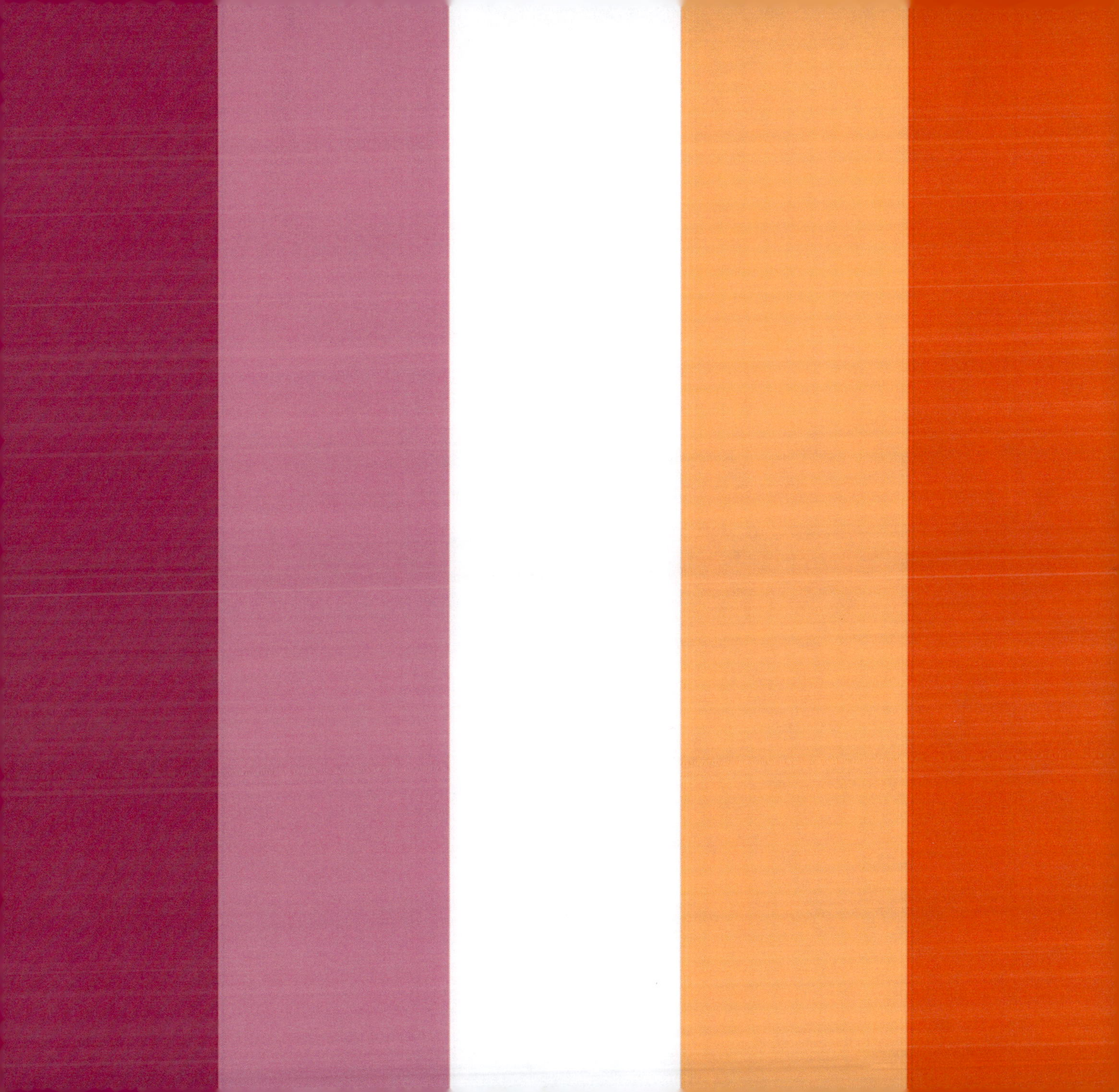

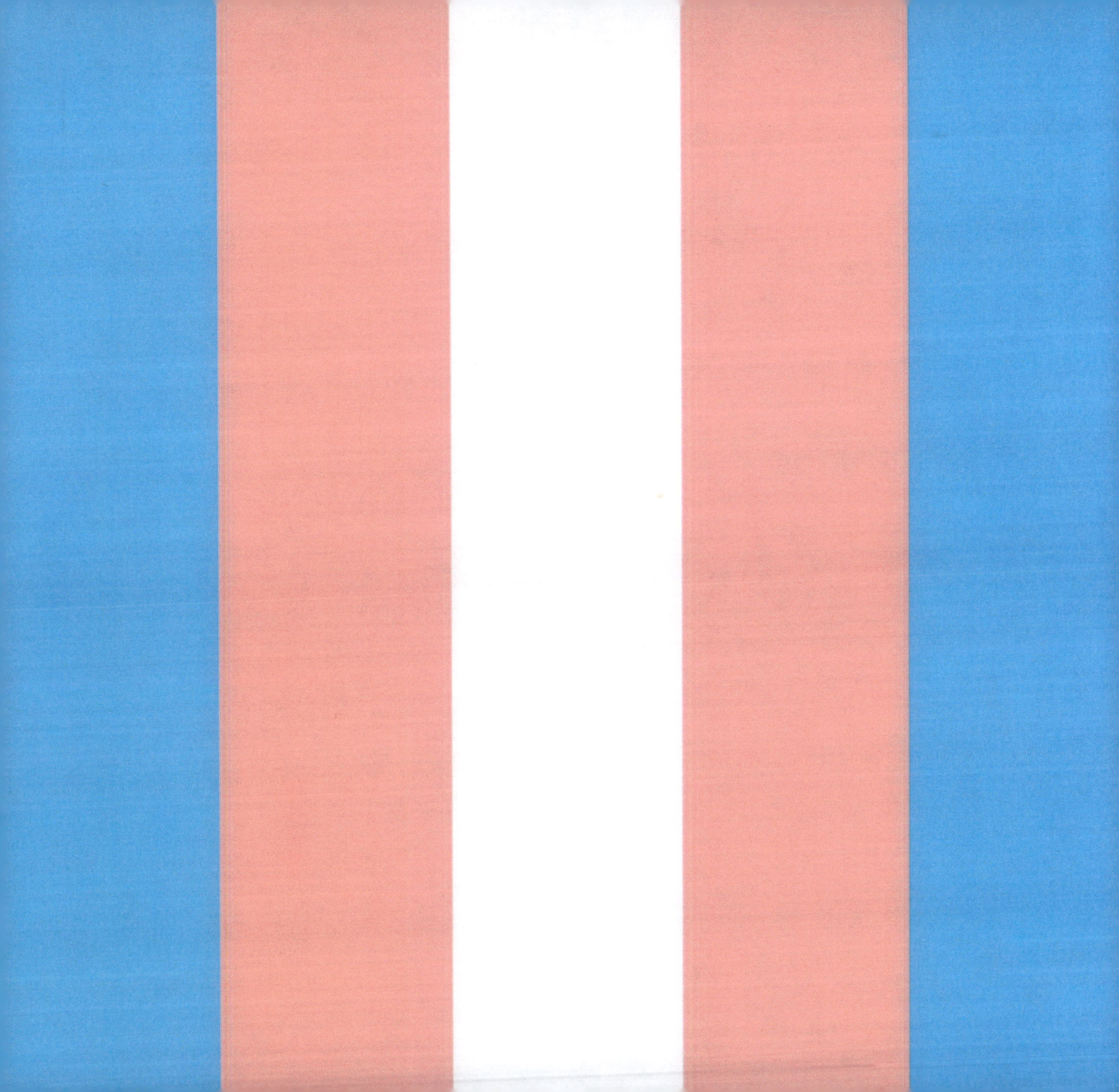

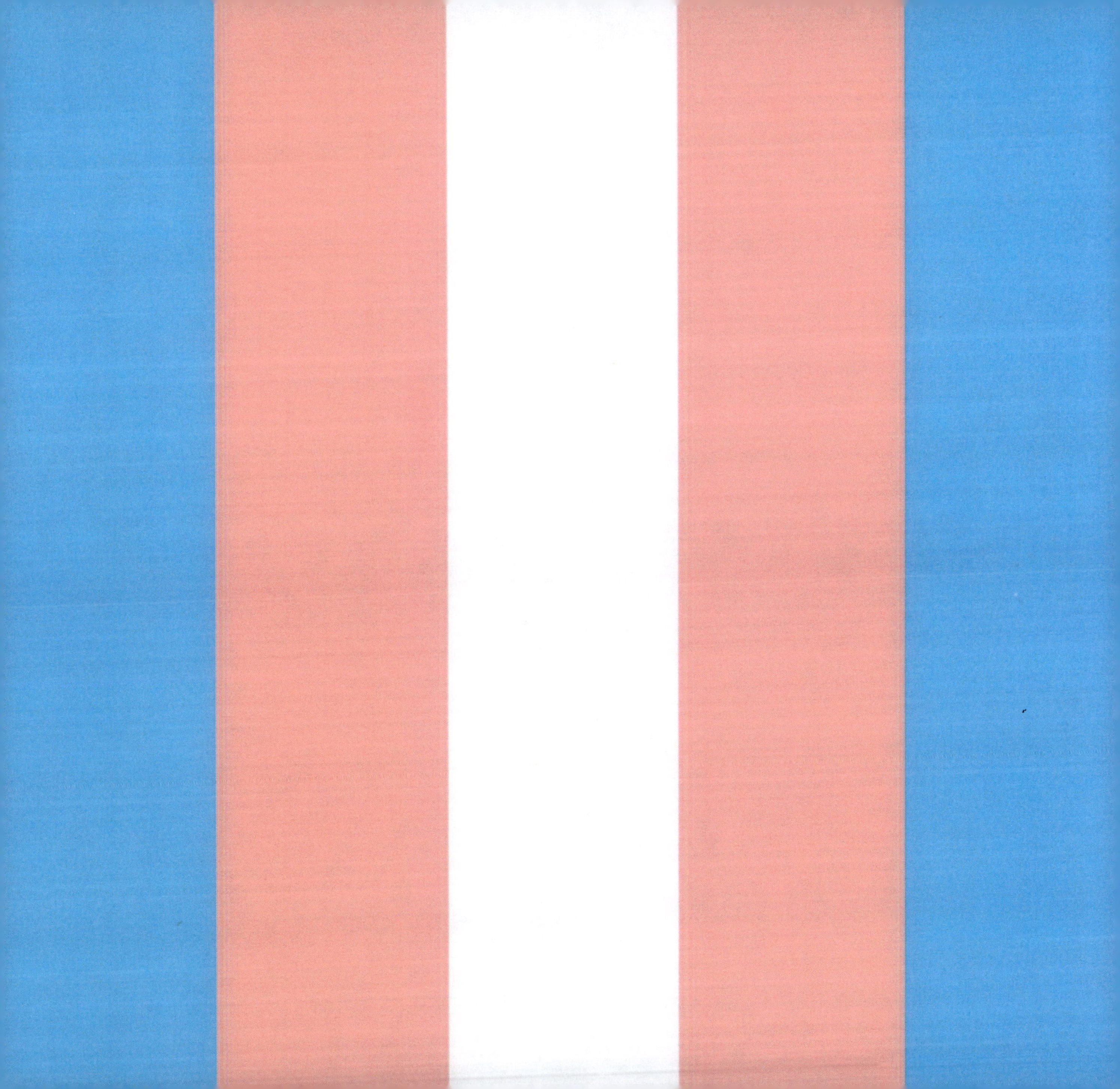

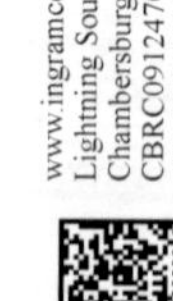

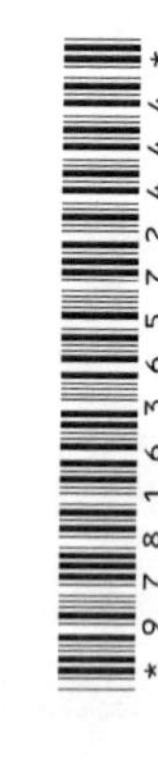
9 781636 572444